The U.S. Capitol

Lola Schaefer

Heinemann Library
Chicago, Illinois

Customer Service 888-454-2279

Visit our website at www.heinemannlibrary.com

Designed by Depke Design
Printed and bound at Lake Book Manufacturing

06 05 04 03 02
10 9 8 7 6 5 4 3

Library of Congress Cataloging-in-Publication Data
Schaefer, Lola M., 1950
        The U.S. Capitol / Lola M. Schaefer.
            p. cm. -- (Symbols of freedom)
        Includes bibliographical references and index
        ISBN 1-58810-178-9
            1. United States Capitol (Washington, D.C.)--Juvenile literature. 2.Washington (D.C.)--Buildings, structures, etc.--Juvenile literature. [1. United States Capitol (Washington, D.C.)] I. Title: US Capitol. II.

F204.C2 S33 2001
975.3--dc21
                                                                            2001001633
Acknowledgments
The author and publishers are grateful to the following for permission to reproduce copyright material:
Cover photograph: Wendell Metzen/Index Stock
p. 5 Terry Why/Index Stock; p. 6 Wally McNamee/Corbis; p. 7 Jay Mallin; p. 8 Bruce Burkhardt/Corbis; p. 10 Joe Marquette/AP Photo; p. 11 Glenn LeBlanc/Index Stock; p. 12 Fredde Lieberman/Index Stock; p. 14 Joseph Sohm/Visions of America/Corbis; pp. 15, 19 Wally McNamee/Corbis; p. 17 Peter Lorber/Corbis; p. 18 Roman Soumar/Corbis; pp. 20, 21, 23, 26, 28, 29 Corbis; p. 22 The Granger Collection, New York; p. 24 Bettman/Corbis; p. 25 Historical Society of Washington, D.C.; p. 27 Hulton-Deutsch Collection/Corbis

Every effort has been made to contact copyright holders of any material reproduced in this book.
Any omissions will be rectified in subsequent printings if notice is given to the publisher.

Some words are shown in bold, **like this.**
You can find out what they mean by looking
in the glossary.

Contents

Center of Government

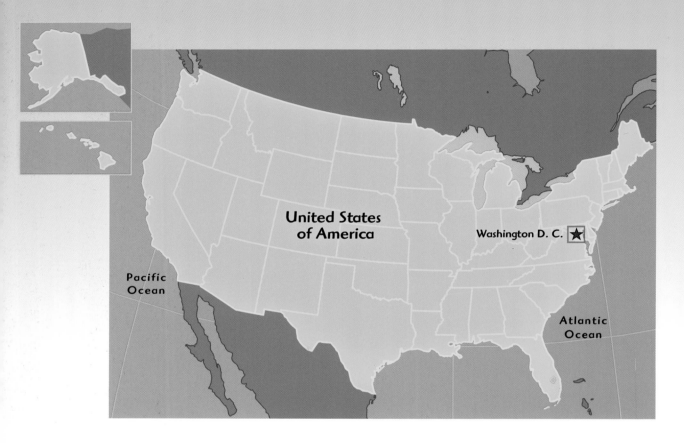

The U.S. **Capitol** is one of the most important buildings in our nation. It is in Washington, D.C., the United States **capital**.

The U.S. Capitol is where **Congress** meets. The building has been a **symbol** of our **government** for 200 years.

What Is Congress?

Congress is the name for all of the men and women who make our country's laws. One part of Congress is the House of **Representatives**. Another part is the **Senate**. Both groups meet in the U.S. **Capitol**.

The House of Representatives and the Senate meet in separate rooms, called "chambers." There are 435 representatives and 100 senators. They come from every state in the United States.

Famous Shape

The U.S. **Capitol** building has a very well-known shape. Many state capitol buildings were built to look like the U.S. Capitol. This is the California State Capitol.

A picture of the U.S. Capitol is on the back of every fifty-dollar bill. The U.S. Capitol building has been used in advertisements, too.

9

Visiting the Capitol

Every year, millions of people visit the U.S. **Capitol**. Tour guides lead visitors through the building. They tell people about the building and how the **government** works.

School children from all over the United States come to the Capitol building. They want to see their government at work. It does not cost any money to go in.

Capitol Hill

Potomac River

National Mall

The U.S. Capitol building is on a hill called "Capitol Hill." It looks out over the Potomac River and the **National Mall**.

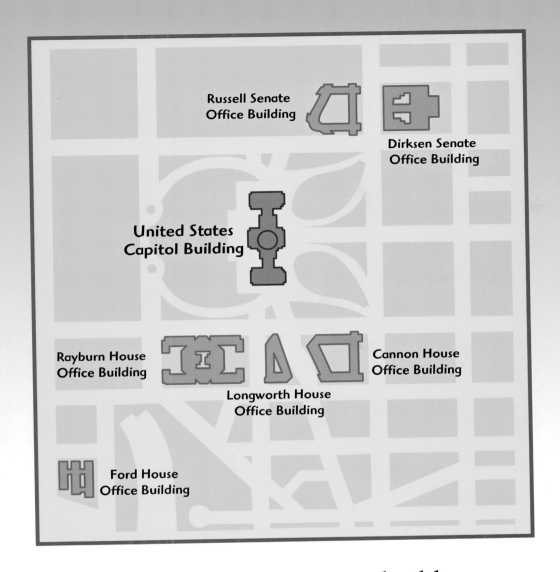

Russell Senate Office Building

Dirksen Senate Office Building

United States Capitol Building

Rayburn House Office Building

Longworth House Office Building

Cannon House Office Building

Ford House Office Building

There are other government buildings on Capitol Hill. Six of them are offices for senators and **representatives**.

Outside the Capitol

The center part of the U.S. **Capitol** is under a **dome**. A **bronze** statue stands at the top of the dome. The statue is called *Freedom*.

The outside of the U.S. Capitol is almost as long as two city blocks. Many steps lead up to the building. United States presidents are **sworn in** on these steps.

Inside the Capitol

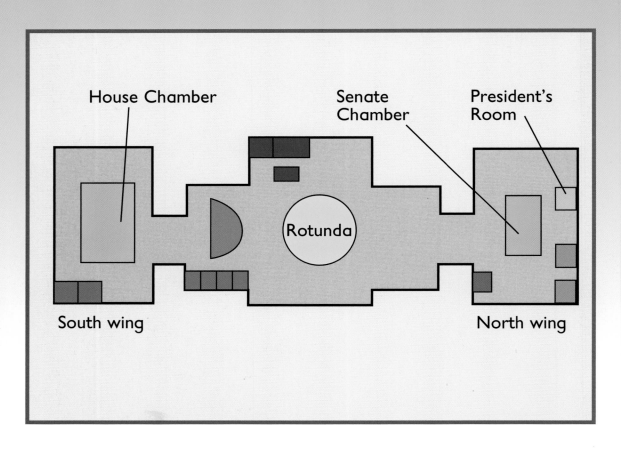

House Chamber

Senate Chamber

President's Room

Rotunda

South wing

North wing

Inside the **Capitol**, the House of **Representatives** meets in the south **wing**. The **Senate** meets in the north wing. Visitors can watch **Congress** from **galleries** above the chambers.

Beautiful artwork fills the Capitol building. Large statues of important Americans stand in the halls. Pictures of U.S. presidents hang on the walls.

The Rotunda

The Rotunda is the large room under the **dome**. It is in the shape of a circle. A large painting of famous people in America's past is in the center of the ceiling.

Many **ceremonies** take place in the Rotunda. It is where the bodies of U.S. presidents sometimes **lie in state**. People can come there to show their respect.

A Home for the Government

In 1790, **Congress** chose land for a new **capital**. This old map shows the land. They called the city "Washington" to **honor** President George Washington.

President Washington laid the **cornerstone** for the **Capitol** in 1793. This old drawing shows how the Capitol building would look.

Slow Work

Building the U.S. **Capitol** was slow work.
Builders always needed more money than
they had. Sometimes work on the building
had to stop for a while.

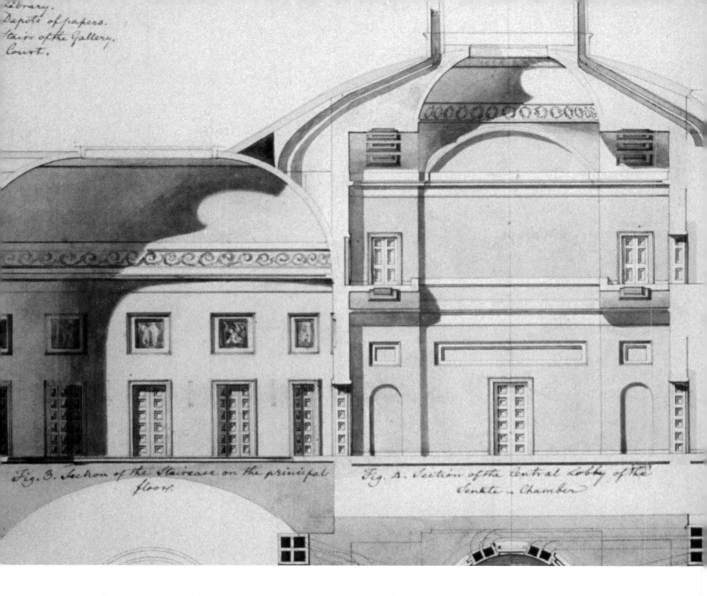

Fig. 3. Section of the Staircase on the principal floor.

Fig. 4. Section of the Central Lobby of the Senate Chamber

The north **wing** was finished in 1800. It was crowded with all the **government** offices and **Congress**. In 1807, the south wing was finished.

Fire!

During the **War of 1812, British** soldiers took over Washington, D.C. They burned many buildings. They burned the U.S. **Capitol** and the **White House.**

Workmen had to rebuild the inside of the Capitol. They replaced some outside stones and scrubbed the others clean. During this time, **Congress** met in an old hotel.

War-Time Capitol

In 1861, the **Civil War** began. The northern states fought against the southern states. Thousands of soldiers lived in the U.S. **Capitol**. It was also a hospital.

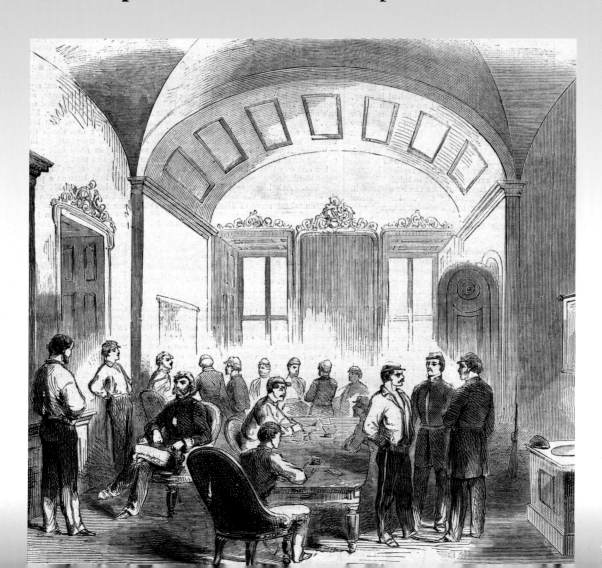

During the Civil War the **cast-iron dome** was placed on top of the building. It weighed as much as 820 elephants!

Modern Times

After the **Civil War**, indoor **plumbing** was put in the U.S. **Capitol**. Workers built a subway train. It took senators and **representatives** from their offices to the capitol.

Today, people can watch what happens in the U.S. Capitol from their homes. People can use televisions and computers to watch the **government** at work.

Fact File

The U.S. Capitol

★ The **Capitol** building is very big. It takes up as much space as four football fields! It has five levels and 540 rooms.

★ The U.S. Capitol used to be heated by fireplaces. Most of them are closed up now, but there are still 139 chimneys on the roof.

★ A statue of Abraham Lincoln in the Rotunda was made by a sixteen-year-old girl.

★ In 1859, **marble** bathtubs were put in the basement of the U.S. Capitol so that members of **Congress** could take baths there. Two are still there today, but no one uses them.

Glossary

British someone or something that comes from Britain

bronze reddish-brown metal that is a mixture of copper and tin

capital important city where the government of a country or state is based

capitol building in which the group of people who make laws for the United States or for a state meet

cast iron mixture of strong metal shaped by pouring into containers called molds

ceremony gathering of people for an important event

Civil War U.S. war in the 1800s, in which northern states fought against southern states

Congress group of men and women who make the laws for the United States

cornerstone first stone of a building that is going to be built

dome rounded top of a building that looks like half of a ball

gallery upstairs seating area or balcony (More than one are called galleries.)

government people and organization that rule a country or state

honor to do something that shows great respect for someone or something

lie in state to put a famous person's body in a public place so that people can see it before the funeral

marble hard, white stone used to make buildings and statues

National Mall large, park-like area of land in Washington D.C. where a museum and memorials are located

plumbing sinks, toilets, and pipes to carry water for them

representative someone who is chosen to speak or act for others

Senate group of lawmakers made up of 100 senators, two from each state

sworn in special event on the first day of a new president's term when he promises to do a good job

symbol something that stands for an idea

War of 1812 war the United States fought against Britain that lasted until 1815

White House house where the President of the United States works and lives

wing part of a building that is added to make the building bigger

More Books to Read

Reef, Catherine. *The United States Capitol*. Parsippany, N.J.: Silver Burdett Press, 2000.

Van Wie, Nancy Ann. *The U.S. Capitol Building*. Laguna Hills, Calif.: Max's Publications, 1994.

Index